CONTENTS

INTRODUCTION

The current Queensland handwriting script was introduced in 1985. Its print style, the Beginner's Alphabet, is based on simple, italic cursive shapes that are easily joined to become Queensland Modern Cursive. Because the capitals remain the same, the two scripts merge easily, so children find cursive writing easier to write as well as to read. Queensland Modern Cursive is designed to be fluent and quick, with maximum legibility.

FOCUS

- carefully sequenced and thorough handwriting program
- progressive revision of cursive joins from two- or three-letter combinations to words
- writing on 8 mm blue lines
- high-interest thematic passages
- large join examples highlight correct direction and rotation
- integrated activities
- joins rocket reference card included
- Theme: inventions.

TECHNIQUE Pencil grip

1. The thumb and the index finger support the pencil while it rests on the middle finger.
2. Child should be able to tap the pencil with the pointer finger while it is supported by the middle finger and thumb.
3. There should be a distance of approx. 2–2.5 cm from the pencil point to the tip of the index finger, 3 cm for a left-hander. Rubber bands are useful markers. Triangular pencil-grips promote correct finger placement and distance.

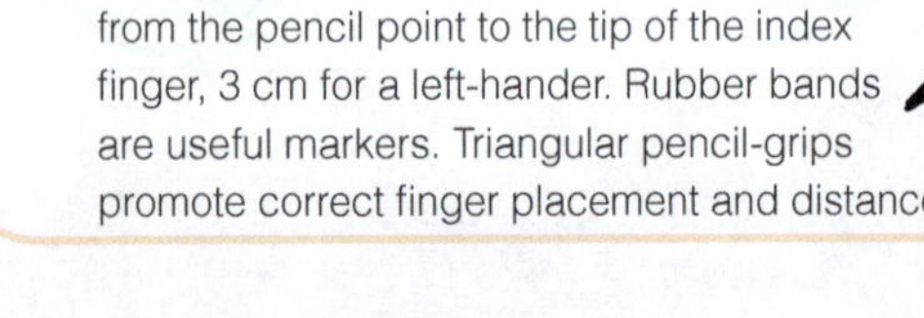

4. Hold pencil barrel up high, near or before the knuckle. Pencil should not rest low in the "web" of the hand.
5. The side of the hand and the little finger act as supports for the whole hand.
6. Unpainted pencils are less slippery.

Posture

Right-handers

1. Keep back straight at an angle of about 30° to back of chair, and keep bottom towards back of seat.

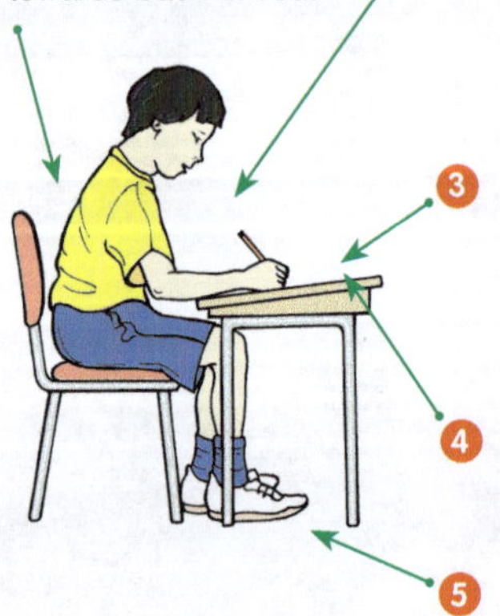

2. Make sure that book or paper is sufficient distance from the edge of the desk to enable most/all of the forearm to rest on the desk. Move book up as child works down the page to maintain this.
3. Table or desk height about level with child's waistline or a bit higher. The weight of the body is supported by the non-writing arm.
4. Sloping desks are ideal, especially for struggling writers.
5. Feet should be flat on the floor.

Left-handers

Left-handers should have their elbow in to discourage a hooked wrist.

Paper position

Left-handed

Right-handed

Right-handed

GENERAL TEACHING TIPS

- Display joins rocket (see reference card on the inside back cover) and the cursive alphabet across the top of the board.
- When commencing writing on 8 mm blue lines, some children with large writing may benefit from writing on every second line in their day-to-day exercise books. This will make their work neater.
- Model handwriting on the board or overhead screen at the beginning of skills lessons.
- Encourage slope.
- Soft, sharp HB pencils are recommended.

Please see further information on the learning features of this book on page 3 and Teacher's Notes on page 63.

LEARNING FEATURES

Clear lesson focus

Large join example to trace, including arrows for correct rotation

Thorough practice from two- or three-letter combinations to words.

High-frequency spelling or reading words used where possible

Invention-theme based non-fiction passages add interest

Space allows teachers to target individual needs

Attractive thematic illustration with speech bubble providing helpful advice. Theme: Inventions

Only possible letter combinations are given

Exits to Rounded Entries
—x

With x, do the exit before you cross it. Drop on the next letter, any letter.

Write under each.

ax ex ix ux ax ex ix ux ax ex

axle exit fixing extra axis excuse

mixture relax expert next sixty exam

luxury explain galaxy index maxi-taxi

Theme sentences:

Wheels are simple, yet ingenious, and the most important mechanical invention of all time. Wheels are found in machines, in clocks, in windmills, steam engines and vehicles like cars and bicycles.

What letters or joins do you need to practise?

1 2 3 4 5 How many points for your handwriting today?

8 Date ___ / ___ / ___

Carefully sequenced program revising all groups: entries and exits to diagonal joins, horizontal joins, pencil lifts, dropping on, sweep up joins and doubles.

Reminder arrows for dropping on to promote good writing habits

Generous spacing for larger writers

Pages with activities in which handwriting can be practised within learning areas across the curriculum

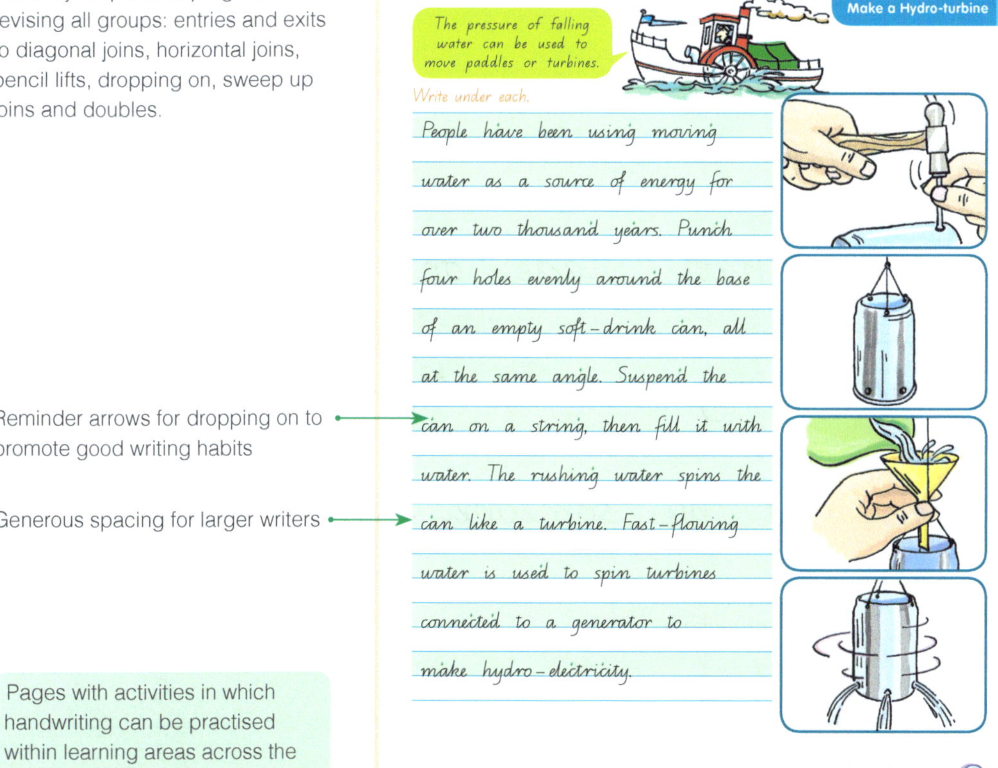
Make a Hydro-turbine

The pressure of falling water can be used to move paddles or turbines.

Write under each.

People have been using moving water as a source of energy for over two thousand years. Punch four holes evenly around the base of an empty soft-drink can, all at the same angle. Suspend the can on a string, then fill it with water. The rushing water spins the can like a turbine. Fast-flowing water is used to spin turbines connected to a generator to make hydro-electricity.

Date ___ / ___ / ___ 27

Sections are colour-coded for easy reference:

- Yellow: skills development
- Blue: sentences
- Green: activities from across the curriculum

A useful joins rocket reference card and handwriting certificate provided

Stretch up at a slippery-slide angle for diagonal joins.

Write under each.

ai ci du hi ly mu ni ty av aw

invite kept myself awful even cycle

until while life still hurt kind

hair river many apart bait built

Theme sentences:

Have you ever wondered who invented sliced bread,
when trampolines were first made or who designed
jeans? Even everyday things like tooth-brushes and
band-aids were invented by someone, some time.

What letters or joins do you need to practise?

How many points for your handwriting today?

Date ..../........../..........

ev

Stretch out to separate letters.

Write under each.

iv ev cu di nu ti av li ey dj aj

link news city event hike money

cure hurry lying chew type buys

dirty living enjoy high keep lunch

Theme sentences:

An invention is a new way of doing something to save time, money or energy and to increase knowledge. They make our lives easier, safer and more enjoyable. Like cars, we could not imagine living without them.

What letters or joins do you need to practise?

Date ..../......../........

an

Make sure your rounded entries look different to your pointed entries.

Write under each.

an am ar en em er in im ir un

amount their climb cents name under

tune ankle animal crust hungry image

grand drum time menu number remind

Theme sentences:

Prehistoric humans tamed fire and invented many tools that allowed them to live as hunter-gatherers and spread across Earth. When early people started to farm, a different set of tools was needed.

What letters or joins do you need to practise?

    1 2 3 4 5 How many points for your handwriting today?

Date .... / .... / ....

Rules:
- Chop off e before adding -ing.
- If there is a vowel before a consonant, double the consonant before adding -ing.
- Two vowels, just add -ing.

Write under the words, adding "–ing" as you go.

begin	watch	swim	cry
sleep	eat	laugh	walk
smile	trust	ride	drop
jump	make	fall	sit
wed	brush	start	write
plant	hop	hide	cough
fire	shut	camp	race
travel	close	wind	feed
read	use	save	stretch
cause	mop	depart	arrive
turn	slide	whip	skate
sweep	trap	believe	dream

Date .... / .... / ....

With x, do the exit before you cross it. Drop on the next letter, any letter.

Write under each.

ax ex ix ux ax ex ix ux ax ex

axle exit fixing extra axis excuse

mixture relax expert next sixty exam

luxury explain galaxy index maxi – taxi

Theme sentences:

Wheels are simple, yet ingenious, and the most important mechanical invention of all time. Wheels are found in machines, in clocks, in windmills, steam engines and vehicles like cars and bicycles.

What letters or joins do you need to practise?

How many points for your handwriting today?

Date .... / .... / ....

it

Finish all the letters in each word, then go back to dot i and cross t.

Write under each.

ie iu in im ir tu ty tw te tu

their kite right giant lift time

sting eight litre centre white title

polite either hint light outside pilot

Theme sentences:

Steam engines burned coal to boil water for steam to power the machines and vehicles of the 1800s and early 1900s, causing a revolution in industry and transport. Eventually steam turbines generated electricity.

What letters or joins do you need to practise?

ne

Stretch out the exit at the angle of a slippery slide to start letter e.

Write under each.

ae ce de he ie ke le me ne te ue

same after them made people ride

place their garden once head under

came take teacher clean table knew

Theme sentences:

Mass transport was invented to carry large numbers of people at one time. Railways from 1830 transported stock, goods and people at much faster speeds than horse-drawn vehicles.

What letters or joins do you need to practise?

    How many points for your handwriting today?

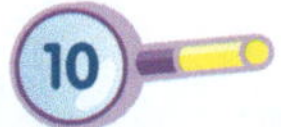

Date ..../........../..........

Modern compasses have two or more magnetised needles that turn freely around a central point inside a container of liquid.

Write under each.

The compass was invented by

Chinese sailors around AD 1100.

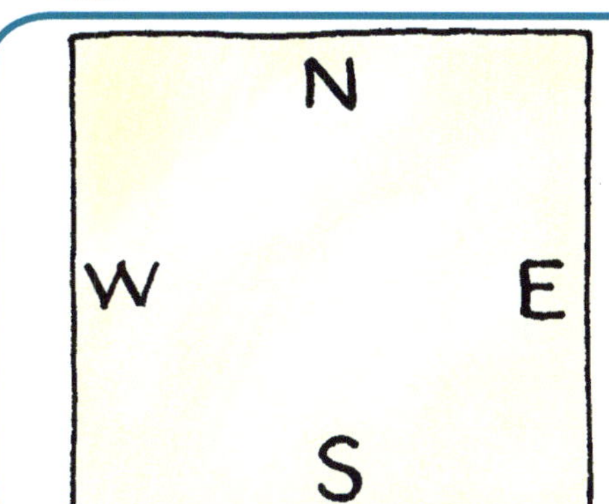

Mark a sheet of paper with

north, south, east and west.

Half fill a clear bowl with water.

Centre it on the paper. Rub a

needle with a magnet many times.

Spear it through a cork and

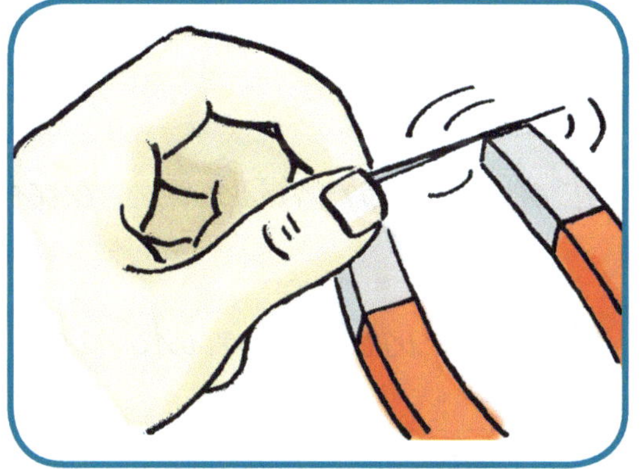

drop it into the water. The

needle will point north – south.

Move the sheet of paper to

match the needle.

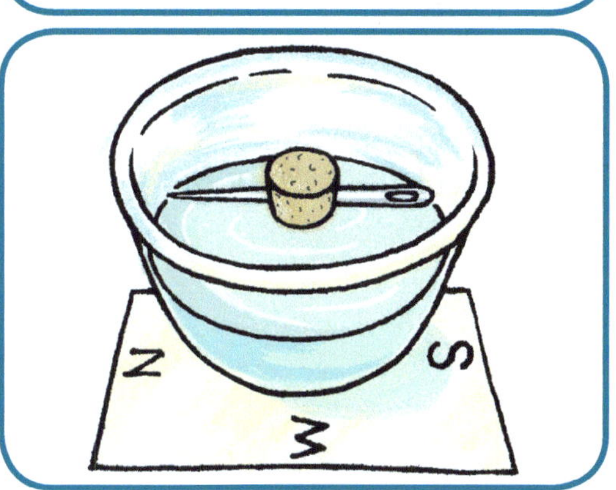

fi

Cross f upwards to join onto the next letter.

Write under each.

fa fe fi fo fu fr fy fl ft fa fe

face fear final form future fries

flew fence finger fold fuel flour

father felt figure friend flower fine

Theme sentences:

Before printing, every book had to be written out by hand, making them rare and expensive. From 1430, Johannes Gutenberg's printing press with movable block letters made knowledge available to all.

What letters or joins do you need to practise?

How many points for your handwriting today?

Date .... / .... / ....

az

Letter z finishes flat like g, j and y.

Write under each.

az ez iz uz az ez iz uz az ez

lazy sneeze fizzy buzz crazy prize

puzzle hazel trapeze size amaze freeze

horizon blaze lizard razor sizzle pizza

Theme sentences:

Cars and bikes revolutionised transport for people every-
where, giving the freedom to travel anywhere. In 1908,
Henry Ford's model T cars were built on a factory
assembly line, which produced a car every minute.

What letters or joins do you need to practise?

Correct entries and open wedges help to tell these letters apart.

n m r

Write under each.

an am ar en em er in im ir un

moment menu minute lemon monitor

chimney many around animal camera

remember morning caravan manager member

Theme sentences:

Candles were expensive, oil lamps were smelly and gas lights gave off fumes. In 1878, Thomas Edison invented a cheap, clean light that could be controlled by the flick of a switch – the electric light bulb.

What letters or joins do you need to practise?

1 2 3 4 5 How many points for your handwriting today?

Date .... / .... / ....

Here are some Australian inventions that have made our world a safer, tastier and better place.

Write under each.

Butter Menthol, Chico Roll, Vegemite, Milo,

Violet Crumble Bar, Hills Hoist, Victa mower,

dual-flush, Stump-jump plough, Race-cam,

winged keel, spray-on skin, baby car capsule.

Theme sentences:

Australians are very inventive. Indigenous peoples

used many different tools to hunt and gather.

Settlers had to be clever to survive. Keeping food

fresh and ploughing fields meant more food.

What letters or joins do you need to practise?

Date .... / .... / ....

u v w

Write under each.

would down never away about gave

wave swim window river even violin

new vitamin weave whenever view

volcano warm universe unwrap wives

Theme sentences:

Many tried to discover the secret of flight. Wilbur and Orville Wright experimented with aircraft theories and designs for years before an historic flight in 1903. Planes improved during the wars.

What letters or joins do you need to practise?

How many points for your handwriting today?

Date .... / .... / ....

Finish the downstroke of r, then curve up to the next letter. Lift if it is too hard.

ri or ri

Try joining, then not joining, from r.

ra ra ri ri ro ro ru ru rn rn

rail ring road burn warm rapid

right robot rusty turn rather risk

rocket ruler earn term rainy rinse

Theme sentences:

In 1826, Joseph Niepce took eight hours to take the world's first photograph. Since then colour photos, 1860, motion pictures, 1895 and digital cameras, 1988 have made photography quick and easy.

What letters or joins do you need to practise?

Date .... / .... / ....

qu

Write under each.

quiet require quad quality squirt

Equator quilt unique quokka liquid

question square quaver earthquake sequence

mosquito quantity barbeque quartz quarter

Theme sentences:

In 1800, Alessandro Volta invented a battery that produced a steady flow of electricity from a chemical reaction between solutions and electrodes. Today's batteries follow his design with modern materials.

What letters or joins do you need to practise?

    1 2 3 4 5 How many points for your handwriting today?

Date .... / .... / ....

A solar cell produces electricity from the sun's rays. They are especially useful for isolated places.

Put a word that makes sense into each gap.

The sun has been producing [1] ____________ for billions of years. As early as 400 BC, [2] ____________ used magnifying glasses to focus the sun's rays on [3] ____________ grass to make fire. In 1953, three scientists, Pearson, Fuller and Chapman, [4] ____________ a solar battery charged by tiny silicon cells that turned sunlight into electricity. The Australian climate is perfect for producing [5] ____________ energy, especially for isolated places. Satellites in space have large black glass panels [6] ____________ with solar cells that change sunlight into electrical [7] ____________. Solar energy will continue to reach the Earth long after [8] ____________ fuels like coal and oil have run out.

Date .... / .... / ....

ao

Letter o joins easily without lifting. Go up to the top centre, then back in an anti-clockwise direction.

Write under each.

ao co do eo ho io lo mo no to uo

colour mouse horse money another below

morning along thought couldn't floor actor

hose koala loud model nobody today

Theme sentences:

The dream of distant speech was realised by Alexander Graham Bell in 1876 with the telephone.

The mobile phone, 1979, was made possible by other technologies: plastics, radio, batteries and the microchip.

What letters or joins do you need to practise?

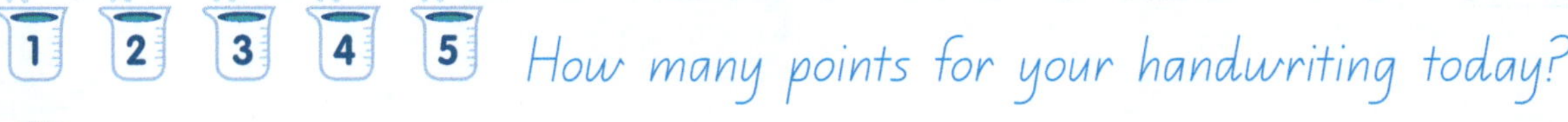

How many points for your handwriting today?

Date ..../........./.........

eb

Curve up to the top of tall letters. Don't lift your pencil.

Write under each.

ab ah ak al ck el et ch cl th

cube think only help until thirty

family always night seventy eighty ninety

February March April July October November

Theme sentences:

Until 1838, everyone had to pay a fee for receiving mail. Then it cost one penny to send a letter, using a circular stamp. Today, through computers, electronic mail, or e-mail, you can give messages instantly.

What letters or joins do you need to practise?

Date .... / .... / ....

If a letter finishes in a clockwise direction, it doesn't join to the next letter.

Write under each.

aba aya ebe eye ibi iyi ubu

ball your blue year baby yellow

before yard bird yawn boat you're

yesterday because young bicycle yourself

Theme sentences:

Sewing began in prehistoric times with the invention of the needle. Before 1851, it took fourteen hours to hand-sew a shirt. Using Singer's sewing machine, it took only an hour. It was truly labour-saving.

What letters or joins do you need to practise?

    5 How many points for your handwriting today?

 Date .... / .... / ....

Write these limericks about teachers. Add your own.

1. There was a Year 6 teacher called Mr Hales,
Who when playing cricket knocked off the bails.
He gave a shout,
The umpire called, "He's out!"
And that was the end of the game for Mr Hales.

2. There was a Year 1 teacher called Mrs Williams,
Who, in the lotto, won millions.
She had a wide choice,
When buying a Rolls Royce,
And driving away called, "Thanks a billion!"

3.

spin

If a letter finishes in a clockwise direction, it doesn't join to the next letter.

Write under each.

asa apa ese epe ipi usu upu

sand paint seal please salad sense

place short pasta pepper stop pick

second people sometimes pineapple station

Theme sentences:

Flushing toilets were first invented for royalty, around 1589. With no drains or running water, it was 200 years before cisterns were placed above toilets. In 1860, Thomas Crapper added an auto-fill float.

What letters or joins do you need to practise?

How many points for your handwriting today?

If a letter finishes in a clockwise direction, it doesn't join to the next letter.

Write under each.

aja aga aza eje ege eze ugu

jelly game zero juice grass zip

zone join gold zoom joke grow

zig-zag journey garden zookeeper goodbye

Theme sentences:

Old newspapers, leaves, corn husks, seaweed, even wet ropes have been used as toilet paper. People thought it wasteful to use clean paper. When toilets came indoors toilet paper that didn't clog pipes was needed.

What letters or joins do you need to practise?

Date .... / .... / ....

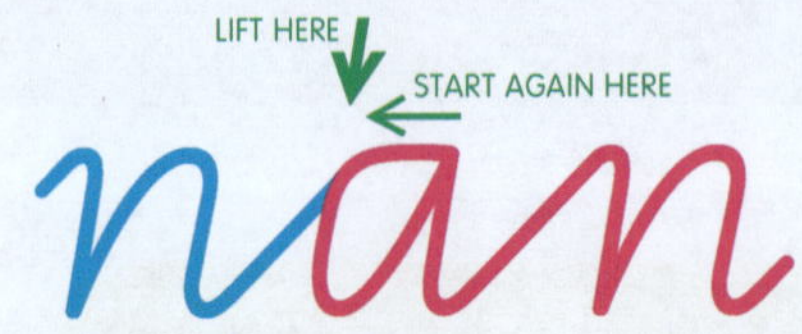

Bring the exit up high, then write the "shoulder" or flat top to meet it.

Write under each.

t talk c cake d daily e each h half

rice easy late make echo hard

native pack became many lunch glad

leaves such dear decide learn music

Theme sentences:

G. Marconi developed the radio, experimenting with radiowaves to send messages through the air in 1896. Making wireless communication over long distances possibly changed the world's news and entertainment.

What letters or joins do you need to practise?

    How many points for your handwriting today?

Date .... / .... / ....

The pressure of falling water can be used to move paddles or turbines.

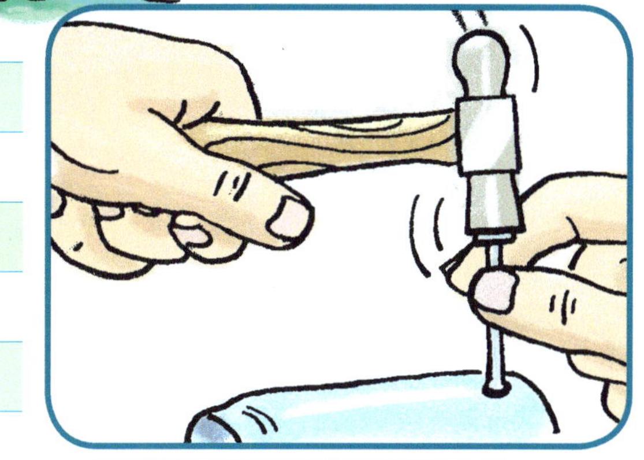

Write under each.

People have been using moving water as a source of energy for over two thousand years. Punch four holes evenly around the base of an empty soft-drink can, all at the same angle. Suspend the can on a string, then fill it with water. The rushing water spins the can like a turbine. Fast-flowing water is used to spin turbines connected to a generator to make hydro-electricity.

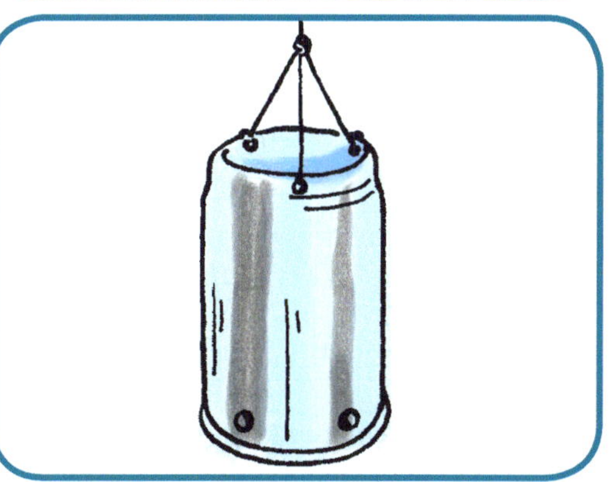

Date .... / .... / ....

a

A high exit at a slippery-slide angle separates the letters before dropping on.

Write under each.

a admit i igloo e equip i idea a aqua

stand laugh request cold thing liquid

coming should young equal send wrong

penguin porridge sequence weight middle

Theme sentences:

With a hot climate and many people living by the sea, swimming and surfing are popular in Australia.

In 1903, the world's first lifesaving club was formed.

In 1906, Lyster Ormsby invented the surf lifesaving reel.

What letters or joins do you need to practise?

How many points for your handwriting today?

Letters that finish near the top go straight across to the next letter.

Write under each.

oa oc od og on op or ou ow oy

story front born crowd doctor brown

corner block atom home stove mouth

mozzie foil chocolate someone group

Theme sentences:

In 1909, Indigenous author and inventor David Unaipon improved shearing clippers. The new clippers cut off more fleece. The removed wool was heavier and sheep only needed shearing once a year.

What letters or joins do you need to practise?

vi ui

The downstrokes on v and w now go straight across. Don't lift your pencil.

Write under each.

va wa vi wi vu wu vo wo vy wy

violin word volume write valley

wishes value woman wrong vine

voyage water vulture wrap vitamin

Theme sentences:

Earle Dickson's wife always had cuts and burns too small for a bandage. In 1920, he cut squares of bandage and stuck them along tape, so she could cut off strips and put the band-aids on by herself.

What letters or joins do you need to practise?

How many points for your handwriting today?

Date .... / .... / ....

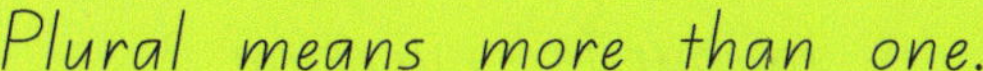

Change each word into its plural form.

cloth	child	knife	monkey
hair	box	baby	cheese
mouse	roof	army	friend
passer-by	hero	dozen	family
holiday	glass	leaf	garden
sheep	cupful	woman	lady
tooth	valley	tomato	city
half	comb	brush	goose
fly	louse	loaf	gas
watch	spoonful	fish	fox

Dip after r to finish it before joining. Lift if it is too hard.

The ute has been voted Australia's favourite invention.

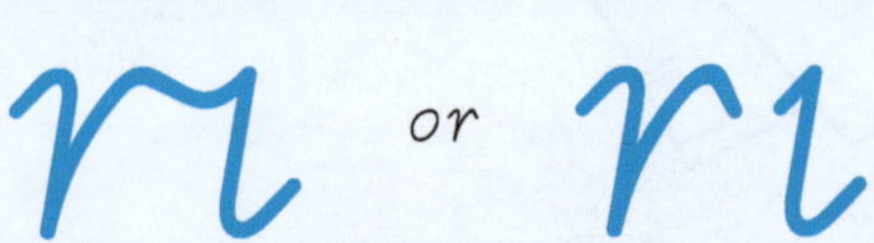

Try joining from r, then lifting after r.

around drive brother friend cruel

drink morning true purple spring

learn through crying germ drum

watermelon Brisbane country surprise

Theme sentences:

In 1933, the ute by Lewis Brandt was two cars in one – a car to take the family out to church on Sunday and the pigs to market on Monday. It had comfy passenger seats and a tray at the back.

What letters or joins do you need to practise?

So many clever people!

Finish with a flick, then drop on a, c, d, g or q.

Write under each.

large	orange	record	grapes	circle
burger	giraffe	lizard	pram	tractor
argue	hardly	grand	guard	parcel
caravan	yesterday	hazard	straw	energy

Theme sentences:

Lance Hill's wife asked him for a better way to dry clothes, so he made a rotary clothesline in 1945. It wound up and down and allowed the clothes to circle in the breeze. Neighbours soon wanted one.

What letters or joins do you need to practise?

oe

Avoid a droopy join to e
—lift after o, r, v, w.

Write under each.

remind very power toes reach west

twelve ready canoe velvet wear does

parents flower every dream surely eleven

ice-cream tomatoes November potatoes seventy

Theme sentences:

When a plane crashes there are often no survivors
to tell what happened, so in 1958 Dr David Warren
developed a way to record engine data and the voices
of the pilots. It is called the "Black Box".

What letters or joins do you need to practise?

How many points for your handwriting today?

 .... / .... / ....

Locate these cities and towns in your atlas.
Print neatly on the map.

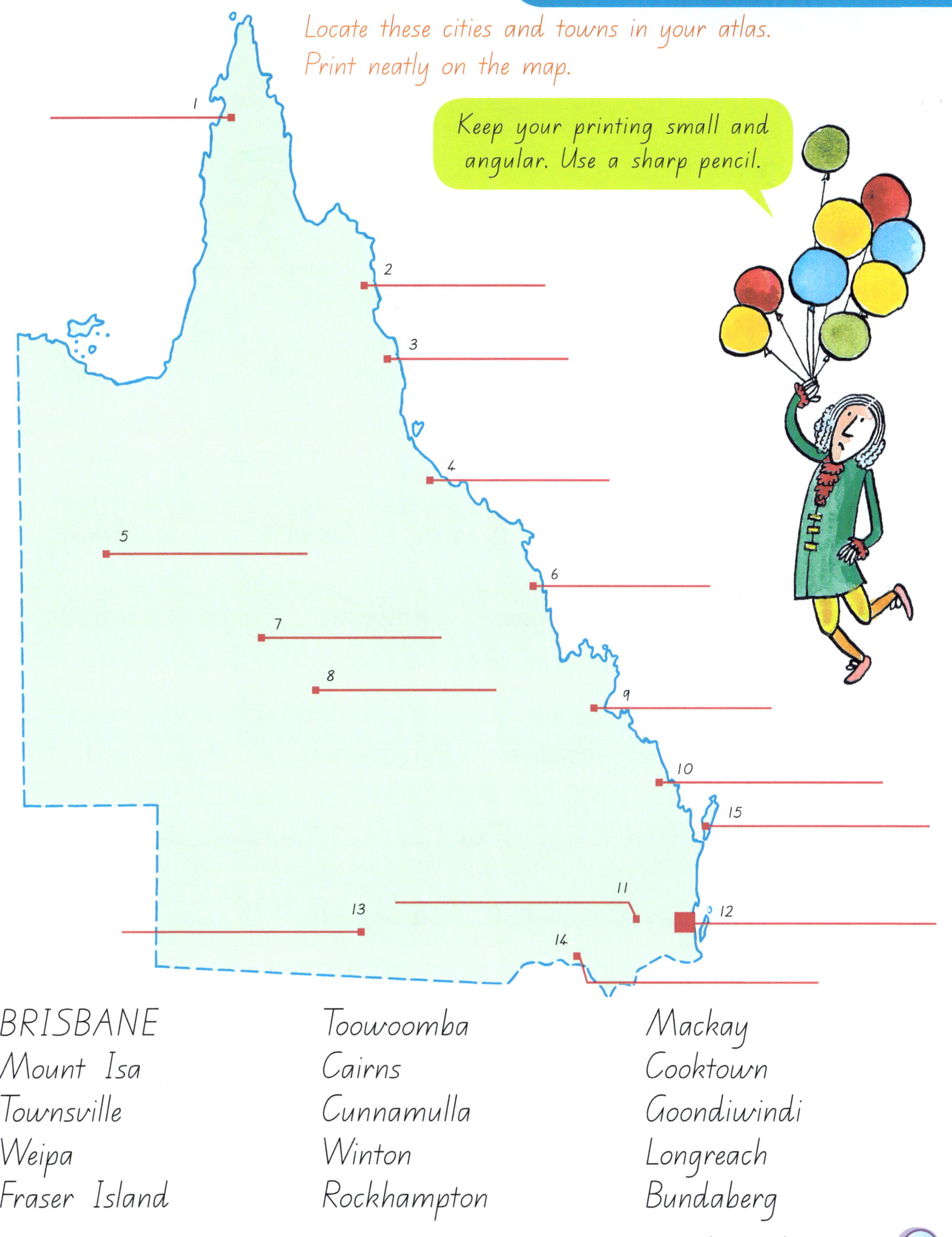

BRISBANE	Toowoomba	Mackay
Mount Isa	Cairns	Cooktown
Townsville	Cunnamulla	Goondiwindi
Weipa	Winton	Longreach
Fraser Island	Rockhampton	Bundaberg

Date .... / .... / ....

ok

Write under each.

ob ol ok ot rb rh rk rt wh wl

joke crawl dirty colour rhyme which

forgot girl artist turkey fourth nothing

airport marbles nobody holiday gold while

Theme sentences:

In 1859, Wilhelm Rontgen discovered a ray that passes through flesh but not bone. X-rays are used to check bone and dental health. In 1973, CAT scans used cameras and computers for 3D x-rays.

What letters or joins do you need to practise?

How many points for your handwriting today?

Date ..../........../..........

A stroke of genius.

Add a long join to the front of f only when needed. The shoulder on f causes the loop.

Write under each.

af ef if of uf rf lf wf af ef

after chief half knife leaf useful

gift selfish deaf careful butterfly

left softball afternoon breakfast thankful

Theme sentences:

In 1928, Alexander Fleming noticed a mould could stop the growth of some bacteria. Penicillin, made from this mould, is now a common antibiotic that destroys bacteria cells without harming the body.

What letters or joins do you need to practise?

Date .... / .... / ....

fife

Use f without a join at the beginning of a word and after a pencil lift. Add a join to f only when needed.

Write under each.

faf fef fif fof fuf frf faf fef fif fof

food seafood fit profit fire bushfire

fall waterfall fin muffin face surface

form platform fund refund fence defence

Theme sentences:

Preserving food in cans was invented by Peter

Durand in 1810. Tinned food was popular with

soldiers and sailors on long trips away from home.

In 1922 Clarence Birdseye developed frozen food.

What letters or joins do you need to practise?

     How many points for your handwriting today?

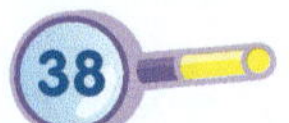

Date .... / .... / ....

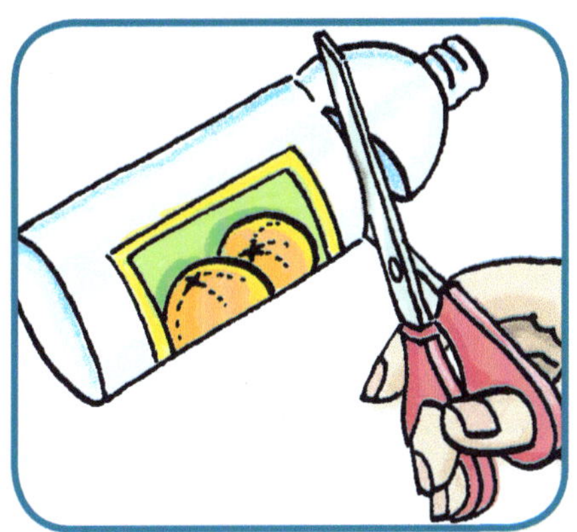

An Archimedean screw is a water-lifting device that has been used for centuries. Cut both ends off a small drink bottle. Wrap a length of clear tubing around it to make a screw shape. Tape. Place one end into a bowl of coloured water, resting it on the edge. Slowly turn the bottle. After a few turns, water will pour out of the top of the tubing. This is named after Archimedes, the scientist.

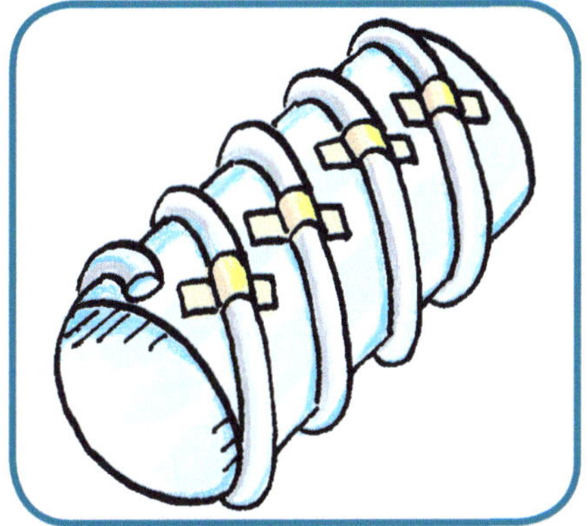

Date .... / .... / ....

Cut the shoulder off s after a diagonal join. This is "modified s" or "s with a join".

as as

Join printed s, then modified s.

as as es es is is us us ts ts ms ms

these answer wasp visitor island

outside wrist house display inspect

August Tuesday Wednesday whistle sunset

Theme sentences:

Plastic is used so much today because it is cheap, waterproof and easily moulded into shapes. It can be coloured or transparent. Leo Baekeland invented the first plastic in 1909. There are many types.

What letters or joins do you need to practise?

1 2 3 4 5 How many points for your handwriting today?

 Date .... / .... / ....

Turn S into S

Write under each.

shake milkshake sand thousand sure measure

scope telescope shop tuckshop serve deserve

son season shoe horseshoe sport transport

still standstill ship friendship search research

Theme sentences:

The trampoline was invented by a gymnast and coach, George Nissan and Larry Griswold, in 1934. Trampolining is now an Olympic sport. Expert trampoliners can bounce to a height of ten metres.

What letters or joins do you need to practise?

Date .... / .... / ....

S

Use printed s at the beginning of a word.

Write under each.

school skates shout start since soap

strong sugar sudden spend speak storm

shadow soccer safety sunrise silent special

sandwich sometimes slippery shoulder southern

Theme sentences:

In 1790, the first rollerskates, by Joseph Merlin, had two wooden wheels in a line and no brakes. Four-wheeled skates were by James Plimton, 1863. Kids put wheels on wooden boards for skateboards in the 1930s.

What letters or joins do you need to practise?

How many points for your handwriting today?

Date .... / .... / ....

It is impossible to say whether more good than bad has come from the inventions of war.

Put a word that makes sense into each gap.

Technological progress is faster in times of war. Each
1 __________ tries to make weapons and machines that
are bigger and 2 __________ than those of the enemy.
Planes improved during both world 3 __________. In
1912, Australian Lance de Mole invented a vehicle that
4 __________ on its own tracks over very rough ground
and could 5 __________ wide trenches. This led to the tanks
of 6 __________ War One. The missiles of World War Two
led to rocket 7 __________ into space. Many things were
invented because of war – radar, penicillin, torpedos, bottled
8 __________ canned food, night-vision goggles, grenades,
sonar, remote-controls and the 9 __________ bomb.

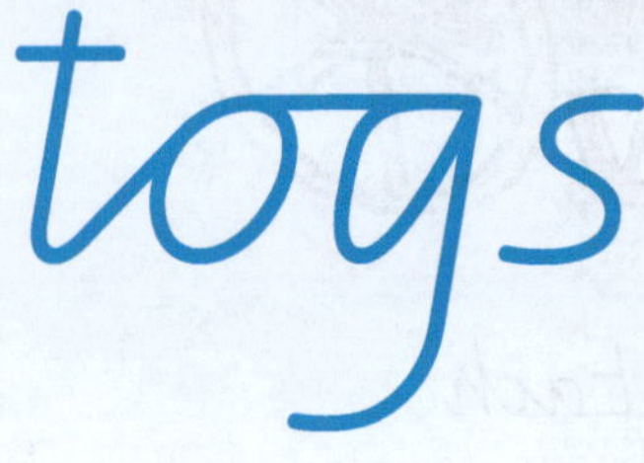

Use printed s after a pencil lift.

Write under each.

system always capsule observe ringside

haystack upstairs website enjoys holidays

monkeys lambs myself valleys seventy-seven

things jigsaw hopscotch joeys mornings

Theme sentences:

Remote-controlled toys are popular. Moving an object from a distance was developed in Germany during World War Two. Bombs were placed inside remote-controlled miniature boats, planes or tanks.

What letters or joins do you need to practise?

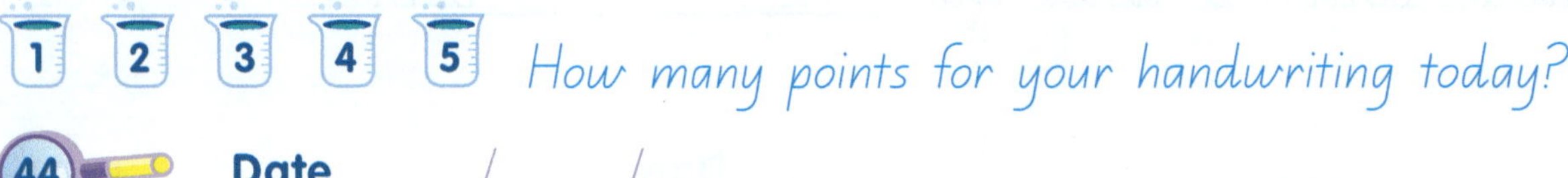

How many points for your handwriting today?

 Date .... / .... / ....

os

Use printed s after a horizontal join. Don't lift your pencil.

Write under each.

os rs ws os rs ws os rs ws os

nurse dosing worst herself almost person

those dinosaur deposit postman cursive

atmosphere yourself parsley pianos cheerios

Theme sentences:

Computers process information faster and more accurately than we can. Computers began just for calculations. The first, in 1944, was as long as four buses. The first computer game was ping-pong.

What letters or joins do you need to practise?

io

Write under each.

Euro demo micro macro info radio

turbo Apollo photo studio Eskimo bingo

rhino jumbo cargo Velcro rodeo lotto

Marco Polo kilo echo choko Pluto cheerio

Theme sentences:

The television is a system of receiving electrical signals from T.V. stations or channels. Since 1953, the aerial on your roof receives the signals and your T.V. converts them back into images and sound.

What letters or joins do you need to practise?

How many points for your handwriting today?

Date .... / .... / ....

When an apostrophe is used to abbreviate words, it is placed where the letter or letters have been omitted, e.g. "there's" is short for "there is".

Write the two words that have been abbreviated.

all's	couldn't	doesn't	hasn't
he'll	I'd	I'm	I've
that's	they'll	won't	you'll
who's	she'd	he's	wouldn't

Abbreviate these words, putting in an apostrophe.

can not	did not	do not	have not
he is	I will	is not	it is
she will	there is	we have	you are
he would	she is	we will	should not

Finish each o in the centre, at the top. Don't lift your pencil.

Write under each.

oooo oooo oooo oooo oooo oooo oooo

hoof tooth roof soon book moon

footpath afternoon kangaroo bandicoot fool

football outdoors cookbook toothless

Theme sentences:

Games and toys are also inventions. Dice were in ancient tombs. We still play old games like chess or cards. Lego, meaning "play well", created its famous bricks in 1949 and has been voted greatest plastic product ever.

What letters or joins do you need to practise?

1 2 3 4 5 How many points for your handwriting today?

Date .... / .... / ....

Write under each.

flood flash flag flex floor

flavour flight flour float fluid

flying flush flower flute flea

floss fleet flatten flick flame

Theme sentences:

Vaccines are made from the same micro-organisms that cause illness, but made weaker or inactive. The body makes antibodies against the illness, boosting immunity for the future – Edward Jenner, 1796.

What letters or joins do you need to practise?

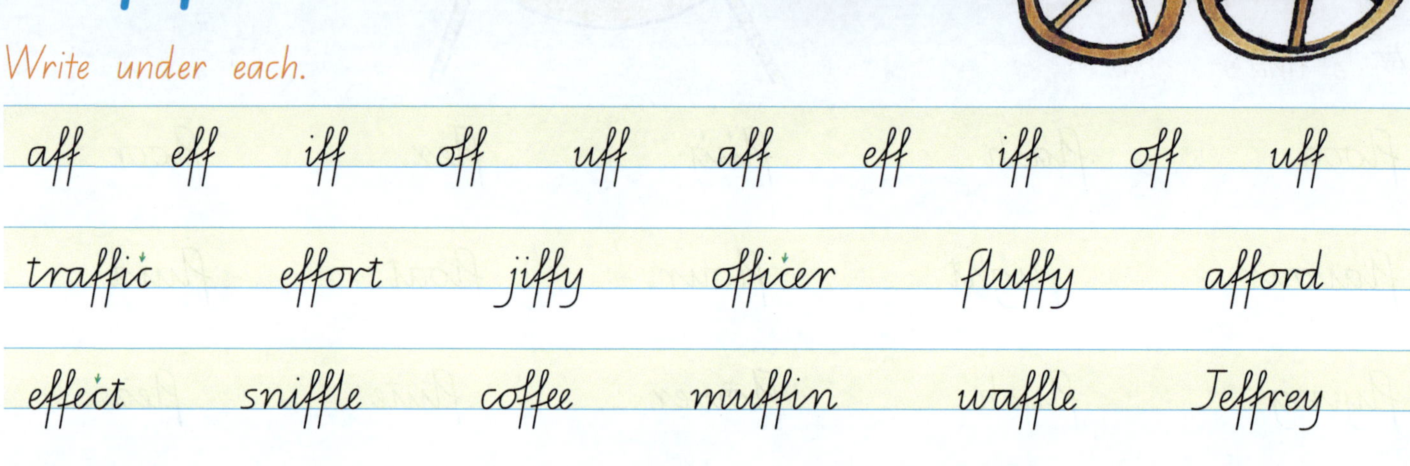

Write under each.

aff eff iff off uff aff eff iff off uff

traffic effort jiffy officer fluffy afford

effect sniffle coffee muffin waffle Jeffrey

shuffle staffroom take-off toffee stuffing

Theme sentences:

Percy Spencer noticed how radar equipment melted chocolate in his pocket, and built the microwave in 1945. Microwaves became small enough for homes in the 1980s. Now almost everyone has one.

What letters or joins do you need to practise?

     How many points for your handwriting today?

Date 

Look after the cents and the dollars will look after themselves.

As you rewrite the passage, put in the missing answers.

Before coins were invented, people swapped goods [1] ________ shark's teeth, cowrie shells, feathers, salt, cocoa beans or furs to [2] ________ for things. The first coins were made in China [3] ________ 100 BC from roughly shaped metal. In other parts of the [4] ________, the first coins were made from lumps [5] ________ silver. By 650 BC silver coins of [6] ________ sizes and weights were made in Turkey. Gold and [7] ________ coins were heavy to carry. In AD 800, the Chinese [8] ________ a lighter form of money – the paper [9] ________. The Chinese had been the [10] ________ to invent paper, 2000 years ago, and the first to print on [11] ________. Australia invented plastic bank notes.

Dip after each r to finish it before joining. Lift if it is too hard.

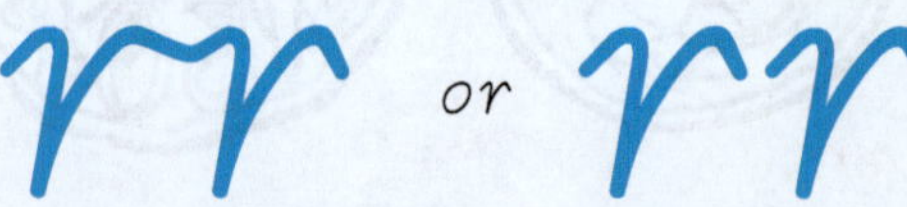

Write under each. Try joining, then not joining after r.

arr arr err err irr irr orr orr urr urr

stirring Ferris wheel strawberry porridge

tomorrow earrings interrupt territory

kookaburra raspberry correcting hurricane

Theme sentences:

In 1957, the first artificial heart was transplanted inside a dog. The heart was made of plastic and driven by compressed air. Many procedures, medicines and ointments have been tested first on animals.

What letters or joins do you need to practise?

How many points for your handwriting today?

Date .... / .... / ....

Stretch the join between double n for legibility. Each n has one wedge.

nn

Write under each.

ann enn inn onn unn ann enn inn

channel winner tonnes funnel-web

goanna tennis beginning connect

spanner cinnamon cunning annual

Theme sentences:

Robots were made in the 1960s to perform repetitive tasks in factories, like welding car pieces. Robots need a computer program, but are strong, accurate and can work in conditions that humans can't.

What letters or joins do you need to practise?

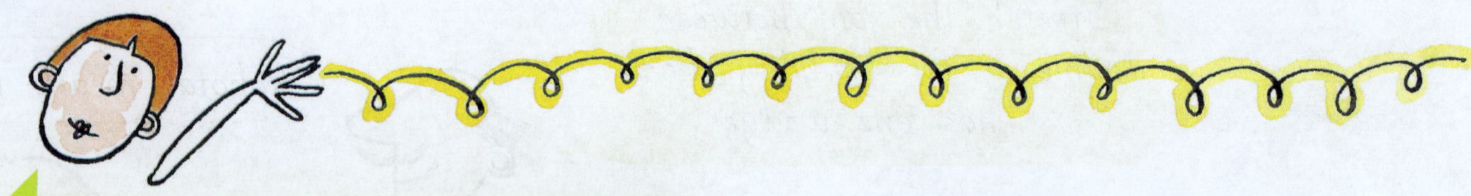

Each m has two wedges. Stretch the join between double m for legibility.

mm

Write under each.

amm emm imm omm umm amm

hammer immune comment summit

grammar dilemma immediate recommend

humming flammable trimmer committee

Theme sentences:

Since the 1960s, ultrasound scanning machines have been used to check a baby growing inside its mother. High-frequency sound waves reflect off soft organs and bounce back as echoes or images.

What letters or joins do you need to practise?

How many points for your handwriting today?

Date 

Make a Vertical-axis Wind Turbine

Wind is a renewable natural resource. A cluster of wind turbines together is called a wind farm.

Write under each.

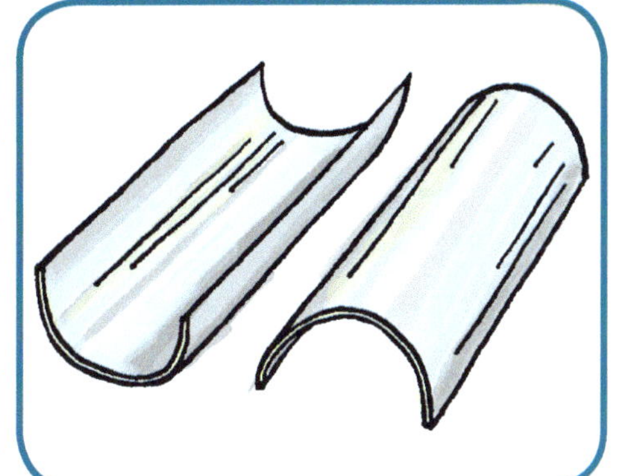

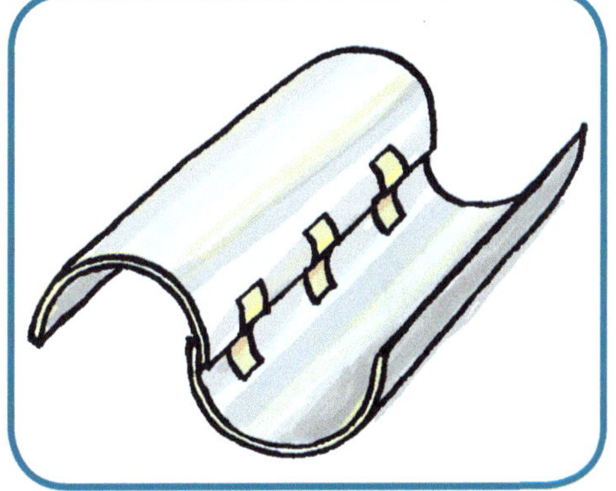

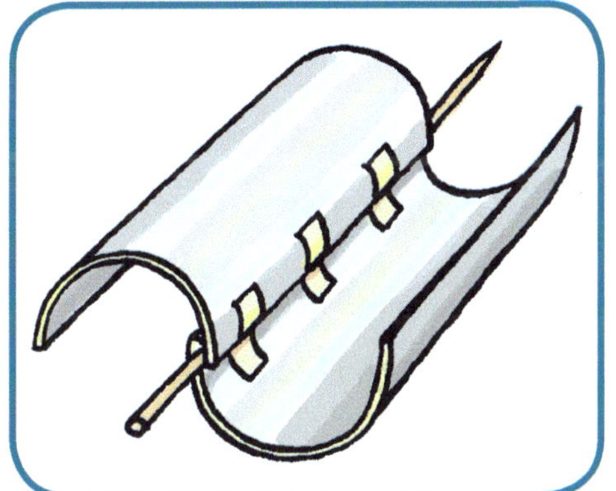

Windmills have been used for centuries to collect wind energy to grind or pump. Make a tube from a bottle. Cut it into two long halves. Form an s-shape and tape together, overlapping by 2 cm. Slide a skewer into the gap. Hold it vertically and blow on it. The windmill spins easily. Vertical-axis turbines are very efficient as they work no matter which way the wind is blowing.

Date ...... / ...... / ......

Stretch out between letters for legible writing.

Oops! I did it again!

ee

Write under each.

eeee eeee eeee eeee eeee eeee eeee eeee

agreed wheel sneeze bleed weekend

meeting pioneer needle greetings between

thirteen fourteen fifteen eighteen nineteen

Theme sentences:

When an organ in the body does not work, it can sometimes be replaced or assisted by a machine. The bionic ear was developed by Australian doctor Graeme Clark in 1978, allowing deaf people to hear.

What letters or joins do you need to practise?

How many points for your handwriting today?

Date .... / .... / ....

vxxi

Give x a high exit, cross it, then the next letter can be dropped on.

Write under each.

sixteen texting mixing extinct luxury

sixty-six exhale taxes fixture deluxe

explain boxing excuse extreme oxygen

relaxing excellent xylophone experiment

Theme sentences:

In 1980, Australian Bruce Thompson invented the dual-flush toilet. Using only five and a half litres for each flush, his invention saves 32 000 litres of water for every Australian household, every year.

What letters or joins do you need to practise?

Date .... / .... / ....

Write under each.

all ell ill oll ull all ell ill oll

spelling million controller lullaby parallel

satellite collage mullet valley propeller

caterpillar umbrella billion pollute bulldozer

Theme sentences:

Japanese and Dutch scientists invented the CD in 1981. It records sounds as microscopic changes in the surface of a plastic disc. These are read by a laser in the CD player and changed back into sound.

What letters or joins do you need to practise?

    5 How many points for your handwriting today?

 Date  .... / .... / ....

Double t can be crossed with one long line.

Write under each.

att ett itt ott utt att ett itt ott

battery glitter butter pattern lettuce

cotton button spaghetti rosette litter

forgotten tutti-frutti pitter-patter wattle

Theme sentences:

Inventors have found ways to capture and use natural power. Solar cells or panels make heat or electricity, windmills can generate electricity and so can the movement of waterfalls, waves and tides.

What letters or joins do you need to practise?

Date .... / .... / ....

ess

Write under each.

ass ess iss uss ass ess iss uss

trespass address kisses fussy dessert

hissing passing essence missing glasses

admission classroom necessary lioness

Theme sentences:

Inventors have worked on sports, devising the rules of games, improving equipment and coming up with clever ideas for having fun and getting exercise. Shoes and uniforms are better, lighter and faster.

What letters or joins do you need to practise?

How many points for your handwriting today?

Date .... / .... / ....

Double s should look like identical twins.

If at first you don't succeed, try, try and try again.

Write under each set or word.

oss oss oss Aussie – cossie fossil glossy

mossie flossing gossip crossword bosses

tossing possible mossy across fossick

glossary losses possum embossed

Theme sentences:

Alfred Nobel, 1833–96, rich inventor of dynamite,

wanted to encourage inventions or methods of

doing things that would make the world a better,

safer place. He left his money for annual prizes.

What letters or joins do you need to practise?

Write a word that makes sense in each gap.

Humans have always [1] ____________ inventors and we're not showing any sign of stopping. In [2] ____________ generation many will say, "There must be a better way than this." Some inventors work alone, others in a [3] ____________. What they all share in common is a passion [4] ____________ exploring ideas, solving [5] ____________ and never giving up until the job is [6] ____________. Most inventions are improvements on [7] ____________ inventions. Many evolved over a long time, others over a [8] ____________ days. Some inventions were inspired by nature: planes by [9] ____________, paper by wasps and Velcro [10] ____________ clinging burdock seeds. Many inventions were chance discoveries, [11] ____________ cornflakes.

1 2 3 4 5 How many points for your handwriting today?

Date .... / .... / ....

TEACHER'S NOTES

Short, daily handwriting lessons are far better than longer, infrequent lessons. Teacher modelling of lesson material on the board to demonstrate the flow of handwriting is essential. The large join example on most pages can be traced. Don't copy directional or dropping-on arrows. All capitals remain printed and separate.

Page

1 Title page and list of contents

2 Introduction

3 Learning Features of Book 5

4, 10, 28 It is useful to liken the angle of diagonal joins to that of a slippery slide to assist correct spacing between letters.

4–8 Two types of entries enhance legibility. Ensure the rounded entries aren't becoming pointed. With "x", the entry, right-to-left stroke and the exit are parallel. It must be crossed immediately, rather than coming back to cross it.

12 The crossbar of "f" is flexible. It is lower when joining to "e" and higher when joining from a top finisher.

14–16 Wedges are approximately two-thirds of the body height.

17, 32 Uncoordinated writers or poor readers of cursive may find "r" difficult to write and prefer not to join from it. Ensure "r" finishes wholly with its downstroke whether it joins or not.

19 Answers will vary. Possible answers include: 1. energy, heat, light; 2. people, humans; 3. dry, some; 4. invented, designed; 5. solar; 6. covered, coated, lined; 7. energy, power; 8. fossil, conventional.

20 The small gap in the large example "o" is to highlight its correct rotation. Do not copy.

21 Sweep up joins have some retracing back down part of the ascenders/ tall letters. These are called covering strokes. No lifting.

21–22, 24–25, 30, 36, 44–45, 48–49, 52, 57–58 "Pencil lift" describes a deliberate stopping within a cursive word and restarting at the beginning of the next letter, to continue that word. It promotes fluency, speed and legibility by avoiding slow, messy looping.

22 Clockwise finishers are letters that finish on the left-hand-side of their form and do not lend themselves to joining. Simply go to the start of the next letter and continue writing.

26–28 Letters with "shoulders" or flat tops are dropped on to avoid a retracing or rocking motion over and back at the top of them. Dropping on is best after a diagonal join to these letters. All drop on letters are based on the "a" shape. An arrow is used to indicate where the exit stops and dropping on is required, throughout the *Write for Queensland* series. Do not copy the arrows.

29, 30, 32 Horizontal joins occur after letters that finish on or near the top blue line: top finishers "o", "r", "v", and "w". The join goes straight across, or dips slightly in the case of "r", to the next letter. The small gap in the large example "o" is to highlight its correct rotation. Do not copy.

33 The dip/flicking after "r" lends itself to dropping on the next shoulder letter, that is, "a", "c", "d", "g" or "q". This is optional and reminder arrows are on this page only.

34 Top finishers don't join to "e", as this does not allow for the correct position of the loop on letter "e".

36 Ensure "r" finishes wholly with its downstroke before sweeping up to the ascender.

37 Modified "f"–a diagonal join to "f" results in a loop.

38 When not joining from another letter, "f without a join" is used, that is, at the beginning of a word, after a capital or after a clockwise finisher.

40–45 Modified "s"–after a diagonal join, the flat shoulder of "s" disappears, leaving a point. Modified "s" should look pointed rather than rounded.

Printed "s" may also be called "s without a join".

43 Answers will vary. Possible answers include: 1. side, country; 2. better; 3. wars; 4. ran, travelled; 5. cross, go over; 6. World; 7. travel, exploration; 8. and; 9. atomic, atom.

48 The small gap in each "o" on the large example is to highlight their correct rotation only. Do not copy.

51 Answers will vary. Possible answers include: 1. like, such as; 2. pay, exchange; 3. in, around; 4. world; 5. of; 6. different, various, many; 7. silver; 8. invented, made; 9. note; 10. first; 11. paper, it.

57 See notes for pages 4–8.

58 See notes for page 21.

60–61 In order to keep double "s" looking right, the first type of "s" determines the second.

62 Answers will vary. Possible answers include: 1. been; 2. every, each; 3. team, group; 4. for, about; 5. problems; 6. done, finished, complete; 7. old, earlier, previous; 8. few, couple of; 9. birds; 10. by; 11. like, such as.

63 Teacher's Notes

64 Pen Skill Award

Inside back cover Reference Card— May be detached and contacted to the student's desk.

____

has worked hard on handwriting.

Assess your own handwriting.

Pressure of Pencil:	Very Good	Good	Need Practice
Pencil Grip:	Very Good	Good	Need Practice
Rounded Entries:	Very Good	Good	Need Practice
Pointed Entries:	Very Good	Good	Need Practice
Diagonal Joins:	Very Good	Good	Need Practice
Horizontal Joins:	Very Good	Good	Need Practice
Dropping On:	Very Good	Good	Need Practice

Teacher's Comments: ____________________________

____

____

____

Date: ____________________ Signed: ____________________